Josette Molland

In Pursuit of Life Essence

Life of a heroine in Resistance Art and the

Will to Endure

Marcia E. Sykes

Table of Contents

Introduction

Josette Molland's life has been impacted by war, dictatorship, and the struggle for freedom. Her relevance stems from her survival and willingness to see the atrocities she witnessed, using art as a powerful tool to depict the reality of Nazi camps.

As one of the few officially recognized Resistance members, Josette's story serves as a living testament to the sacrifices made by individuals who stood up to tyranny. Her achievements as an artist, as well as her role in the creation of forged papers for the Resistance, illustrate a varied individual who, despite a horrible tragedy, found methods to resist and contribute to the cause.

In 1943, Josette Molland, a bright art student, took the life-changing decision to join the Resistance. Making bogus papers for the Dutch-Paris underground network became her hidden mission, both liberating and dangerous. Her encounter with Suzie, a tall young Dutch lady, sparked her involvement in a network that would become a lifeline for Jews, Resistance members, and Allied airmen seeking refuge.

Josette's experience unfolded under the shadow of the Gestapo, culminating in her capture by the legendary "Butcher of Lyon," Klaus Barbie. Her capture and subsequent trials are a key episode in the story of her resistance, laying the groundwork for the horrible battles she would face in Nazi camps.

Purpose of This Book

The book provides insights into Josette's involvement in the Resistance, shedding light on lesser-known aspects of resistance efforts, such as the role of artists and document forgery. It also emphasizes the power of artistic expression as a form of testimony, looking into the intersection of art and history.

The novel humanizes historical figures by delving into Josette's early life, relationships, and personal problems, fostering empathy and understanding for the subtleties of individual lives in the midst of war. It also promotes awareness and alertness by depicting Josette Molland's story as a call to action, urging you to remain vigilant against injustice and actively work for a just and compassionate society.

Josette Molland's Early Life and Background

Josette Molland's story begins in the central French city of Bourges, where she was born on May 14, 1923, into the Molland family. Her father, Gaston Molland, had a hardware store in Lyon, a city that would later play an important role in Josette's life. The family's beginnings in Bourges provided a sense of stability and community, laying the framework for Josette's early years.

Growing up in the Molland household, Josette experienced the typical ups and downs of childhood. The Molland family house was surely filled with the comforting aromas of her mother Raymonde's cooking, as well as the echoes of her father's hardware company stories. These early years created a sense of familial warmth and resilience in Josette, qualities that would later characterize her in the face of great sorrow.

However, the tranquility of her upbringing was abruptly disrupted by the looming clouds of war. The fear of German domination hung over France, casting a shadow on Josette's fate in ways she could not have foreseen during her naive years in Bourges.

Josette's artistic talents blossomed throughout her time at Lyon's École des Beaux-Arts. This prestigious art school became the furnace in which her artistic skills were honed and refined. The city's vibrant cultural scene, along with the supervision of qualified instructors, provided Josette with an environment conducive to creative development.

Here, she immersed herself in the world of shapes, colors, and emotions, developing skills that would later be critical in both her resistance acts and her artistic goals as a Nazi camp survivor. Lyon, known for its silk industry and creative heritage, served as a canvas for Josette to create the first brushstrokes of her artistic identity.

Josette's creative career took a practical turn when she found herself working in the silk industry. In her early twenties, she was already making a name for herself as a designer for Lyon's silk weavers. Josette's drawings were used to embellish cloth woven on Lyon looms, highlighting a convergence of art and industry. Little did she know that her artistic powers would soon be used in a far more dangerous mission, one that would take her beyond the realm of silk and into the heart of resistance against occupation.

The weight of the Resistance's covert efforts would eventually supersede the heavy woolen clothing made by silk weavers, which had previously served as a source of income and artistic expression. As the German occupation grew, Josette's early skills in the silk industry influenced her eventual profession as a document forger, where she used her creative ability to create phony papers for the covert activities of the Dutch-Paris underground network.

Josette Molland's early life is woven into a tapestry of creativity, familial ties, and the looming shadows of war as she progresses from an art student to a key contributor to the Resistance. The foundations laid at Bourges and Lyon would stand the test of time, sustaining her through the turbulent years ahead as she embarked on the path of resistance against Nazi persecution.

Taking the Bold Step to Join the Resistance

In the spring of 1943, Josette Molland's life took an unexpected turn when, after a session at Lyon's École des Beaux-Arts, she was approached by Suzie, a tall young Dutch lady. Josette had no idea that this encounter would propel her into the heart of the Resistance and lay the groundwork for her remarkable journey.

Suzie, a key member of the Dutch-Paris underground network, identified Josette as a potential recruit with tremendous skill. The network had become well-known for its daring activities, which included moving Jews, Resistance members, and Allied airmen over borders to safety in Switzerland. Josette's creative ability and proclivity for caution made her an ideal candidate for a work that required both imagination and secrecy.

Despite the dangers, Josette accepted Suzie's request because she felt a sense of duty and wanted to help oppose the German occupation. This decision marked the start of a secret chapter of Josette's life, in which every action has consequences and the stakes were nothing short of life and death.

Joining the Resistance meant Josette willingly entered a perilous atmosphere where danger lurked around every corner. The gravity of her actions became clear when she accepted a post that involved manufacturing forged documents and delivering them to the Dutch-Paris network. The risks were enormous, with the discovery by the Gestapo carrying a possible death sentence.

Josette's dedication to the cause enabled her to navigate the perilous environment of occupied France with a determination that went beyond personal safety. Fabricating bogus documents was more than just a job; it became a form of resistance in and of itself. The act of providing persons with means to avoid persecution and even death demonstrates Josette's unwavering belief in the justice of her cause.

Josette's role in the Resistance was not limited to covert operations; her creative abilities became a powerful weapon against oppression. She contributed significantly to the fabrication of phony papers by using her skills. She cut rubber stamps from municipal halls and prefectures, resulting in laissez-passer certificates that allowed people to travel quietly throughout the restricted zones.

The intersection of art and resistance in Josette's actions is a testament to the multifaceted nature of her efforts. Her paintings would later serve as a visual tribute to the crimes she witnessed, while her meticulous forgeries allowed many people to escape the invaders' iron grip. This mix of inventiveness and subversion exemplifies the resourcefulness that defined the Resistance's efforts.

The coming war against the Gestapo became a reality on the sad morning of March 24, 1944. A furious "Boom Boom Boom! Open up! Police!" shattered the illusion of safety. Two Gestapo agents, joined by a member of the French auxiliary Gestapo squad, entered Josette's environment.

The interrogation took a bad turn when Klaus Barbie, the famed "Butcher of Lyon," presided over the questioning. Barbie, who was responsible for the death of Resistance commander Jean Moulin, was well-known for his brutality. Josette and her friend Jean were tortured and intimidated, but Josette, stubborn and determined, maintained a stony silence. Despite the awful suffering, her refusal to disclose information protected the network she had been a part of.

The events of that day were a watershed moment in Josette's life. Her tenacity under interrogation displayed the unbreakable spirit that would get her through the horrors of Nazi deportation and imprisonment in the months that followed. The encounter with Klaus Barbie, albeit awful, served as a testament to Josette's dedication to the cause and refusal to be broken by tyrannical powers.

Survival In Nazi Camps

When Josette Molland was apprehended by the Gestapo, the most dreadful chapter of her life began. The arrest on March 24, 1944, signaled the start of a horrific journey. The interrogation sessions under the harsh glare of Klaus Barbie and his companions were more than just an attempt to obtain information; they were a horrible display of power intended to break the spirit of the resistance.

Josette's unwillingness to disclose information, as well as her stoic silence in the face of torture, became a testament to her resilience. Her commitment to the cause was unshaken despite the physical and psychological anguish she endured. The heavy toll she sustained during these sessions set the tone for the more serious trials that awaited her in the Nazi camps.

On August 11, 1944, Josette Molland boarded a train with 102 other women bound for Ravensbrück, a well-known women's concentration camp. The journey itself was a terrible introduction to the deplorable conditions of Nazi transportation, foreshadowing the horrors that awaited them.

Josette was tied at the ankle and placed on a mound of coals as punishment for attempting to escape during the journey. The physical and mental toll of the journey mirrored the ferocity of the administration she had become entangled with. Ravensbrück, known for its strict discipline and severity, provided the grim backdrop for Josette's strong will to persevere.

Josette's trip through the Nazi camp system began when she was sent to Holleischen, a forced labor camp in what is now the Czech Republic. Holleischen, like Ravensbrück, had its own horrors, as prisoners were subjected to arduous labor, harsh conditions, and the constant threat of death.

In the face of unimaginable tragedy, Josette Molland's soul did not break; instead, it transformed into a force of resistance within the confines of the camps. Josette assumed command at Holleischen after learning that the work included making armaments for the Germans. Her call for a prisoner's strike echoed the collective desperation and determination of those around her.

"If we all refuse, they can't kill all of us!" Josette said, comprehending the power of collective resistance. The walkout was met with brutal repercussions; convicts were forced to stand at attention for hours, and anyone who fell was shot immediately. The guard protecting the woman, a common-law prisoner convicted of murdering her family, had the power of life and death over them.

Josette's valor extended beyond organized opposition. In a stunning act of survival and negotiation, she drew a portrait of the guard, earning her favor. This little yet devastating depiction of humanity in the midst of dehumanization highlighted Josette's tenacity and adaption in the face of the most difficult circumstances.

The wheels of liberation began to turn as Polish resistance members entered the camp on May 5, 1945, only days before Germany was defeated. The Germans lined up against the wall to face justice for their crimes. When the Americans arrived, the French ladies, survivors of unfathomable sorrow, sang "La Marseillaise" while distributing food and preparing cars to drive them away.

For Josette, liberation was a bittersweet experience. The physical shackles had been removed, but the emotional scars remained deep. The excitement of release was mingled with grief for those who had died, friends, and colleagues who had not survived the horrors of the camps.

The journey back to Lyon was a somber return to a world forever changed. Reunited with her mother, Josette had the challenge of reintegrating into a culture still dealing with the aftermath of war. Her physical survival was successful, but the psychological toll was enormous. Every day was a reminder of the tragic happenings in the camps, and the memories tortured her as she struggled with how to live a "normal" life after such dreadful tragedies.

Josette Molland's survival in Nazi camps is more than a story of tenacity; it is a testament to the human spirit's ability to resist, even in the face of systematic dehumanization. Her journey through capture, torture, and the horrific conditions of the camps exemplifies the fortitude that emerges from the darkest corners of history. The liberation, while a joyous occasion, marked the start of a lifelong journey of healing, reflection, and the search for a future free of the bonds of the past.

Life of Josette Molland After the War

Following her liberation from Nazi camps, Josette Molland embarked on the difficult process of rebuilding her life in postwar France. As evidence of her perseverance, she opened a clothing business in Lyon. This activity represented not just a professional desire, but also a return to normalcy in a society torn apart by violence and sorrow.

The clothing business became a clear representation of Josette's desire to advance. It provided a space for her to weave new threads in her life, bringing not just apparel but also a story of survival and hope to a nation emerging from the shadows of war.

Josette's postwar years unfolded in a tapestry of connections, each thread adding to the rich pattern of her existence. During one pivotal period, she married a Polish officer, forging ties that crossed national boundaries. This partnership represented not just a personal commitment, but also a link between different wartime experiences, raising Josette's knowledge of the global effects of conflict.

As life took an unexpected turn, Josette fell in love again with Serguei Ilinsky, an exiled Russian prince with whom she married for the second time. Serguei's history and experiences added depth to Josette's already diverse life story, emphasizing the richness that comes from embracing several cultures and histories.

The postwar period introduced Josette to new chapters and geographical views. A move to England marked a turning point in her life, providing opportunities for new beginnings and exploration. The reasons behind Josette's move, whether personal, professional, or greater, were critical to her life's development.

Josette eventually settled in Nice, France, where she now lives permanently. The sun-kissed sands of the French Riviera provided the backdrop for her last years. Settling in Nice not only provided a peaceful environment but also represented the resilience inherent in her personality - tenacity that sought solace and beauty even after facing the worst parts of human history.

Amidst the winds of change, Josette experienced a fantastic reconnection with her artistic beginnings. Her passion for art resurfaced during the postwar period. This creative reawakening was more than just a return to prior interests; it also served as a therapeutic outlet for articulating the depths of her experiences.

Josette's creative pursuits grew beyond personal expression to include restoration work. Playing a role in the preservation of cultural heritage, particularly the restoration of the Russian Orthodox Basilica in Nice illustrated the symbiotic relationship between her personal journey and wider contributions to the cultural fabric.

The years following the war were not without difficulty. Josette, like every other human navigating life's challenges, had personal struggles. Whether it was the loss of loved ones, the weight of memories from Nazi camps, or the complicated issues of adjusting to a world irreparably torn by war, Josette's life path embodied the human experience in all of its aspects.

Despite the difficulties, there were small but significant accomplishments that helped create her story. She carried medals from her time with the French Resistance as visible reminders of her contributions and persistence. The classification as an officially recognized Resistance member highlighted not just her individual story, but also the collective memory of those who stood up to oppression.

Josette's life evolved over time into a living testament to the human spirit's unwavering tenacity. Her 100th birthday in May 2023 is a watershed moment in her life, a testament to her strength, adaptability, and unwavering commitment to bearing witness to history.

Josette Molland's postwar life is a narrative of regeneration, endurance, and the unwavering pursuit of life's rich tapestry. From the founding of a clothing firm in Lyon to marriages spanning diverse cultural landscapes, her life exemplified the mentality of forging on despite previous traumas.

The move to England and eventual residence in Nice emphasized the dynamic nature of her journey, which occurred against a backdrop of many landscapes, indicating the complexity of her experiences. The rediscovery of her artistic passion, along with repair work, demonstrates a critical link between personal expression and cultural asset preservation.

Throughout the postwar years, Josette faced personal challenges, but her achievements rang louder. The medals she wore, her designation as a Resistance member, and the centennial celebration were more than just individual accolades; they were echoes of a life integrally linked to the collective narrative of resistance against oppression.

As we look at Josette Molland's postwar journey, we see a life that embraced change, valued diversity, and, most importantly, never lost the weight of history. Her story transcends time, serving as an eternal testament to the human ability to rebuild, rediscover, and persist in the face of our shared history's worst moments.

Josette Molland's Artistic Legacy

Josette Molland embarked on a spectacular artistic enterprise in the late 1980s that would become an enduring legacy: a series of paintings depicting her harrowing experiences in Nazi camps. Motivated by strong anxiety that her message was not reaching the younger generation, she chose a visual medium to transcend the limitations of language and impart an emotional understanding of the atrocities she had witnessed.

These paintings, totaling 15, depict the terrible realities of life in Ravensbrück and Holleischen. The paintings were rendered in a naïve, folk-art style, devoid of emotion, enabling the ferocity of the settings to resonate. One image, labeled "The Big Search," portrays a humiliating search for a naked woman, while another, titled "Collecting the Dead at Night," reveals the horrific consequences of the camp's circumstances.

Josette carried these paintings with her whenever she interacted with audiences, particularly young people in schools. The decision to use art as a medium was deliberate; she translated her experiences into a visual tale that transcended time and language, ensuring that the horrors of the past were not forgotten.

Josette Molland's decision to embrace art as a means of communication was driven by a desire to bridge the age gap and convey the gravity of the Holocaust to younger audiences. Her paintings were more than just depictions of personal grief; they were also compelling instruments for education and memory.

According to her own words, "I use them to explain to young people in schools what the human race is capable of, hoping that my testimony awakens their vigilance and encourages them to act every day, so they don't have to live what I did." Her mission to educate through art reflects her deep understanding of the power that comes with visual storytelling, which can arouse empathy, instill awareness, and act as a living testament to the consequences of oppression.

Josette's desire to share her feelings via art had a significant impact on succeeding generations. The stark honesty of her paintings, along with her personal experiences, left an indelible impression on anyone who heard her speak. Her paintings' visual language communicated effectively across cultural and linguistic boundaries.

Her work with schools and presentations at French educational institutions established her as a living link to a time of history that is rapidly fading from direct memory. The impact on students was enormous, as they were presented with the awful reality of the Holocaust not through distant tales, but directly from a survivor who witnessed the horrors.

Beyond the classroom, Josette's reputation as an officially recognized Resistance member lent credibility to her message. Her impact extended beyond the canvas, with her prizes serving as real symbols of resistance. The recognition by French officials solidified her place in history, highlighting the importance of individual narratives in shaping community memory.

Josette's creative influence extended beyond personal expression and Holocaust memorial. Her work on the restoration of the Russian Orthodox Basilica in Nice demonstrates a commitment to preserving cultural heritage and nurturing the collective memory of many cultures.

Josette contributed significantly to the restoration project by collaborating with her second husband, Serguei Ilinsky. This project brought together her artistic ability with a desire to preserve physical representations of the cultural and religious past. The basilica, with its rich tapestry of iconography and architecture, served as a testament to the continued legacy of faith and endurance.

Josette's involvement in restoration work was more than just the careful repair of physical structures; it was an extension of her drive to ensure that the stories embedded in these cultural treasures were preserved for future generations. Her work transformed her into a history guardian, a steward of the physical remnants that link the present to the past.

Josette Molland's artistic impact extends beyond the canvas and is a living testament to the power of art as a vehicle for education, remembering, and cultural preservation. Her series of paintings developed out of a strong concern for the transmission of history and became portals into the deepest depths of human experience. She used visual storytelling to not only remember past misdeeds but also to encourage vigilance against future injustices.

The impact of her efforts on future generations, as well as her recognition as a Resistance member, highlighted the long-term importance of individual narratives in shaping our understanding of history. Josette's artwork and personal experiences in classrooms and lecture halls inspired students to confront the harsh realities of the Holocaust, establishing a common desire to prevent such tragedies from occurring again.

Josette's efforts to renovate the Russian Orthodox church in Nice add to her creative legacy. In preserving cultural heritage, she served as a link between the past and the present, ensuring that the narrative enshrined in these physical monuments endured over time.

When we consider Josette Molland's artistic legacy, we see not only a survivor but also a storyteller who used the language of art to convey the incomprehensible. Her paintings, lectures, and restoration work together form a mosaic of resilience, remembering, and a profound commitment to ensuring that the echoes of history live on in the collective knowledge of future generations.

Josette's Last Years and Legacy

Reaching 100 is an uncommon and significant milestone, a testament to a life marked by accomplishments, hardships, and the unavoidable passage of time. Josette Molland reached this great age in May 2023, surrounded by memories of her rich and powerful experience. The celebration of her centenary was more than just a personal success; it was a community recognition of a life that spanned a century in human history.

The celebrations surrounding Josette's 100th birthday were a mix of happiness and contemplation. Friends, supporters, and those whose lives she had affected gathered to remember a woman who had not only escaped the horrors of Nazi camps but had also become a beacon of hope, a living link to a turbulent past. With congratulations and shared stories, Josette's centenary became a collective celebration of tenacity, courage, and the enduring strength of the human spirit.

On February 17, 2024, Josette Molland died in Nice, the city that had become her home in her later years, as the pages of time turned, putting an extraordinary life to a conclusion. The news of her departure reverberated across the communities that had been touched by her presence - a lady who had witnessed and withstood the darkest parts of history, leaving an indelible mark on everyone who had crossed her path.

Her death marked the end of an era, the loss of a live link to the dreadful days of World War II; nonetheless, the significance of her life persisted beyond the grave. In her final moments, Josette bore the weight of history, the memory of endurance, and the immense impact of a life dedicated to bearing witness to the past.

Josette Molland's retirement was not a quiet farewell; rather, it reflected the immense impact of her life. Her funeral, held on February 28, 2024, in Nice, was a somber but dignified ceremony presided over by the mayor, Christian Estrosi. The full military honors bestowed upon her were more than just a ceremonial gesture; they recognized her accomplishments as a member of the French Resistance.

The military medals reflected Josette's legacy as both a survivor who had witnessed the horrors of war and a resistance member whose bravery had been publicly honored. The severity of the occasion matched the gravity of the history she represented, honoring a woman who had stood up to injustice and emerged as a beacon of fortitude.

As we reflect on Josette Molland's final years and legacy, her biography emerges as a tapestry fashioned from strands of courage, perseverance, and a steadfast commitment to giving witness to history. Her life was more than just a personal story; it was a living testament to the collective strength of people who opposed tyranny.

The joy of her centenary and the sadness of her death were times of reckoning with the complexity of her legacy. Josette Molland was more than just a Nazi camp survivor; she was also a storyteller who used art, lectures, and personal experience to ensure that historical lessons remained relevant throughout time. Her paintings, which served as a visual journal of sorrow, were transformed into educational and commemorative instruments.

Her personal experience was given governmental validation when she was recognized as a member of the French Resistance. The medals she wore were more than just symbols of personal bravery; they represented a collective resistance that refused to be silenced. The full military honors during her funeral were a societal acknowledgment of the obligation owed to those who stood up to Nazism, a recognition that extended beyond the individual to encompass the larger narrative of resistance.

As we reflect on the ongoing impact of Josette Molland's life and narrative, we are confronted with not just the history she lived but also the history she helped shape. Her legacy lives on in the minds of those who heard her speak, saw her paintings, and felt the indomitable spirit of a lady who rose from the depths of human history with courage, elegance, and an unwavering determination to ensure that the echoes of the past are never forgotten.

Josette Molland's name will go down in history as one of those who witnessed the unfathomable and turned personal sorrow into a rallying cry for recall and vigilance. Her story asks us to confront harsh realities from the past, recognize the enduring impacts of hatred, and accept the responsibility of ensuring that the legacy of resistance lives on in the collective awareness of generations to come.

Conclusion

Josette Molland's life was nothing short of extraordinary, with a storyline that included the tumultuous environment of World War II, incarceration in Nazi camps, postwar reconstruction, and a desire to preserve history through art. Josette was born on May 14, 1923, in Bourges, France, and her early years were marked by the everyday routine of a loving family. Little did she know that the shadows of war would soon wash over her existence.

Josette joined the French Resistance in the spring of 1943, driven by a strong sense of purpose. Her artistic talents became a weapon in the fight against persecution when she created fake documents for the Dutch-Paris underground network. On March 24, 1944, she was abducted by the Gestapo, tortured, and imprisoned by Klaus Barbie, the infamous "Butcher of Lyon."

Josette was sent to Ravensbrück and Holleischen, where she endured beatings, and hunger, and witnessed the deadly toll of typhus. Despite all odds, she lived and returned to France during the liberation. Her post-war life included opening a clothing business in Lyon, marrying a Polish officer, moving to England, and eventually settling in Nice with Serguei Ilinsky.

Josette's determination goes beyond her aspirations. In the late 1980s, motivated by a fear that her story would be forgotten, she began creating a series of paintings depicting her time in Nazi camps. This artistic activity, along with her discussions and contributions to the renovation of the Russian Orthodox Church in Nice, transformed her into a living link between the past and the present.

Josette Molland's life story is a testament to the indomitable spirit of the human soul. Her perseverance in the face of unthinkable catastrophes, her unwavering will to oppose injustice, and her contributions to history via art and activism establish her as a major character.

Her survival in Nazi camps was more than a matter of luck; it was a testament to her resilience and resolve to survive, even in the darkest of circumstances.

Josette's valor in joining the Resistance, fabricating bogus documents, and facing the brutality of the Gestapo displayed her commitment to a larger cause. Her perseverance in the face of bodily and emotional agony exhibited determination that could not be broken. Through her paintings and talks, she became a storyteller who saw history, ensuring that the lessons learned from her experiences were passed down through generations.

Josette's efforts to renovate the Russian Orthodox Basilica in Nice demonstrated her commitment to preserving cultural heritage. When dealing with physical remnants of history, she became a curator of the stories contained in the architectural and artistic fabric of the past. Her efforts extended beyond personal goals, demonstrating her confidence in the community's obligation to ensure that the echoes of the past are not lost to time.

Josette's story became indicative of a larger narrative of the battle against fascism as she was a recognized member of the French resistance. The medals she carried were more than simply symbols of personal bravery; they were tangible reminders of a shared struggle against injustice. The full military honors performed at her funeral were a societal acknowledgment of the devotion paid to those who, like Josette, had fought the forces of evil with unwavering determination.

In the final chapter of Josette Molland's incredible life, there is a powerful desire to remember, learn, and act. Her impact extends beyond the pages of history, serving as a living testament to the long-term consequences of hatred and the human spirit's ability to endure. As we reflect on her story, we recognize the critical importance of learning from her experiences in the ongoing pursuit of justice and compassion.

Josette's persistence in adversity shows us that even in the most dire circumstances, the human spirit can persevere and triumph. Her commitment to justice, as seen by her participation in the Resistance and her artistic talents, is a guiding light in our shared quest for a world free of injustice. Her narrative encourages us to address harsh historical realities and stand up to those who seek to perpetuate injustice.

As we navigate a world still dealing with the ghosts of the past and the complexities of the present, Josette Molland's legacy serves as a beacon of inspiration. Her paintings, lectures, and life stories are not relics of a bygone era; rather, they are living reminders that the quest for justice and humanity is an ongoing journey. The call to remember is more than just a commemoration of the past; it is a commitment to creating a future in which history's lessons guide our collective actions.

We commemorate Josette Molland not just as a woman, but also as a symbol of resistance, resilience, and the unwavering pursuit of a just and compassionate society. Her memory encourages us to be vigilant against the spread of hatred, to oppose forces that undermine human dignity, and to strive for a future in which the indomitable spirit of individuals like Josette shines for years to come. Josette Molland's enduring legacy is unquestionably reflected in the ongoing pursuit of justice and humanity.